TAI CHI
FOR SENIORS

DISCOVERY PUBLISHER

©2014, Discovery Publisher

All rights reserved.
No part of this book may be reproduced in any form or by any electronic or mechanical means including information storage and retrieval systems, without permission in writing from the publisher.

Author : Dejun Xue
Editor : Adriano Lucchese

DISCOVERY PUBLISHER

616 Corporate Way, Suite 2-4933
Valley Cottage, New York, 10989
www.discoverypublisher.com
books@discoverypublisher.com
facebook.com/DiscoveryPublisher
twitter.com/DiscoveryPB

New York • Tokyo • Paris • Hong Kong

TABLE OF CONTENTS

Comments on Tai Chi for Seniors	7
1. Preparation	19
2. Starting Tai Chi	25
3. Catch Bird's Tail	29
A. Ward Off	29
B. Pull Back	35
C. Squeeze	38
D. Double Push	41
4. Single Whip	51
5. Taking Hands Attack	65
6. White Crane Spreads Wings	81
7. Right Push and Brush Knee	89
8. Playing Guitar	99
9. Right Push and Brush Knee	105
10. Left Push and Brush Knee	113

11. Right Push and Brush Knee   121

12. Playing Guitar   129

13. Side Punch and Straight Punch   135

14. Closing   149

15. Cross Hands   157

16. Ending Tai Chi   163

TAI CHI
FOR SENIORS

COMMENTS ON TAI CHI FOR SENIORS

Tai Chi Quan is a Chinese word. *Quan* means fist and *Tai Chi Quan* is a martial art based on the theory of *Tai Chi*; although, usually, *Tai Chi Quan* is simply called *Tai Chi*.

Yin and yang in harmony constitute the state of *Tai Chi*. *Tai Chi for Seniors* is an exercise developed from the traditional *Tai Chi (Tai Chi Chuan)* with emphasis on the harmony of *yin* and *yang*.

This is a symbol of *Tai Chi*. The light portion of the symbol is *yang*, which represents the characteristics of heaven. The dark portion of the symbol is *yin*, which represents the characteristics of earth.

Tai Chi for Seniors employs relaxation. After *Tai Chi* start, the body should be held erect, naturally. The height of the body should remain stable, fluctuating neither up, nor down. The head should be positioned as if you were holding up a weight. Do not lean either forward nor backward; otherwise, the chest will be stressed. Do not puff up the chest, but relax it naturally. If the shoulders are raised, they will be stressed; therefore, do not raise the shoulders, but relax them naturally.

Do not raise elbows up too high, nor too close to ribs. Drop the elbows naturally. Tuck the buttocks in; otherwise, the internal organs will be tense. Relax the wrists. Do not stretch the palms of your hands, but allow them to open naturally, like fans. The tips of your fingers should never be higher than the eyebrows. If the hands are too high, the ribs will be stressed. Do not stretch the fingers, but relax them naturally.

When holding a fist, the fist is loose, forming a hole with the fingers. When pushing, force does not originate from the hands, but from the body. Do not stress the lips. Do not frown. Do not grit your teeth. Relax the face. The tongue touches the roof of the mouth. Any saliva forming in the mouth, is swallowed. While the entire body is relaxed, the mind focuses on the flow of energy around the body in response to breathing and movement. The movements progress smoothly without pause. From the preparation of a movement through to the end, there is no starting or stopping point; all postures are connected smoothly. Before the true end of a posture, another posture begins.

Tai Chi for Seniors employs rhythm. The movements alternate between the accumulation and release of energy. During the accumulation of energy, the body contracts, with the arms and hands brought close to the body; during the release of energy, the body expands, with arms reaching out, pushing or punching.

Accumulation of Energy: Yin (阴)

Release of Energy: Yang (阳)

To accumulate energy is *yin*; to release energy is *yang*. When *yin* and yang are in harmony, the accumulation and release of energy are in balance.

The alternation of *yin* and *yang* is rhythmic, like the alternation of night and day. To be rhythmic, the movements encompassing a large distance are faster than the movements encompassing a smaller distance, so that the duration of time used to accumulate energy is equal to the duration of time used to release energy.

Time [Accumulation of Energy: Yin (陰)]

═══

Time [Release of Energy: Yang (陽)]

Correspondingly, the duration of time for inhalation is equal to the duration of time for exhalation. Usually, inhalation and exhalation takes about eight seconds, each. The slower the movement, the deeper the breath; therefore, if you want to breathe deeper, you can increase inhalation and exhalation to twelve seconds, each. If you wish to spend less time practicing *Tai Chi*, you can inhale and exhale for only four seconds, each. Usually, a complete cycle of breathing in sixteen seconds is most comfortable and beneficial to your health.

Tai Chi for Seniors is thorough, more like a slowly moving tree, rather than a fast running car. While the tree is being blown by the wind, its whole body moves, with the exception only of its roots, which are still. In contrast, a car is not rooted in the ground at all, but while it is running, its internal parts, (seats, dashboard, etc.) are still. While practicing *Tai Chi for Seniors*, the feet touch the ground fully and firmly, like the roots of a tree. Try to keep your hips facing forward. The lower body, from hips to feet, is like the main trunk of a tree. Turning the shoulders to the left or right, is like swaying the branches of a tree around its trunk. In this way, the spine twists. Each section of the spine, the spinal cord and the internal organs, move. The spine acts like an axle, with the shoulders turning around it. The force comes from the muscles surrounding the spine, rather than from the shoulders. Then, the shoulders bring movement to the arms, the arms bring movement to the hands, and the hands bring movement to the fingers.

The order of movement is: shoulders first, arms second, hands third, fingers last. Fingers follow hands, hands follow arms, arms follow shoulders. The move is slow, but not still. All joints at hips, shoulders, elbows, wrists and fingers are moving completely, and rotate in different directions, not just in one direction. The movement of the arms is not only 'extension and contraction', but rotation, as well. The forearms rotate around the elbows and the hands rotate around the wrists, counter-clockwise or clockwise, as demonstrated in the dragon dance. There is almost no one-dimensional movement; most of movements are three-dimensional. The lungs are flushed thoroughly. The slow rhythmic movement facilitates deep breathing.

During inhalation, the lower abdomen contracts and the diaphragm raises up. The fresh air filling the lungs, reaches the upper lobes, and the internal organs are pressed gently. When the body is twisted, turning to the left or right side, the internal organs are pressed harder. During exhalation, the lower abdomen and diaphragm expands and the carbon dioxide is released. The internal organs are relaxed. With slow motion and relaxation, the *qi* (mind-focused point) moves progressively, like fluid flowing around the whole body, reaching the four terminus areas: the tips of the toes, the tips of the fingers, the top of the head and the tip of the tongue.

Tai Chi for Seniors is flexible. The footsteps may be flexible. You do not have to move your feet exactly as I am doing. You may move one of your feet back, forward, to the side or upward, while I am moving my foot forward. You may move one of your feet forward, while I am stepping back with my foot. Just remember to alternate the weight on your feet.

By keeping footsteps flexible, you can practice *Tai Chi for Seniors* indoors, outdoors and even when travelling, without being limited by space.

The postures may be flexible. You do not have to move your hands exactly as I am doing. Your hands may be pointing to a position higher or lower than my hands, because we are practicing for health, not for fighting. However, you should follow the basic principles of *Tai Chi*.

The basic principles are:

• Relax: relax the chest, shoulders, elbows, wrists and fingers. Keep the head erect and aligned with the spine and tuck in buttocks.

• The spine acts as an axle: stand with both feet firmly touching the ground, like the roots of a tree. During movement, the hands follow the arms, the arms follow the shoulders, and the shoulders rotate around the spine.

• Three external coordinations: the head coordinates with the buttocks, the elbows coordinate with the knees and the hands coordinate with the feet.

• Three internal coordinations: vision, breathing and mind are coordinated.

• Five elements: move forward, back, turn to left, turn to right and keep body straight.

• The height of the body is flexible: if you feel tired, your postures may be high. If you feel energetic, your postures may be very low. But the height of body should be stable, unwavering, from *Tai Chi* start to end.

• The tips of the fingers are never higher than the eyebrows.

The order of movements is flexible, and you can practice *Tai Chi* any time it is convenient for you. You may practice just one portion of *Tai Chi for Seniors*, or only one single posture; however, in order for it to be beneficial to your health, practicing *Tai Chi* at least thirty minutes a day is necessary.

TAI CHI
FOR SENIORS

1. PREPARATION

- Be calm for a few seconds. Stand straight.
- Relax your face and shoulders.
- Drop your hands naturally at your sides.
- Relax the chest and hips.

- Begin to inhale.
- Move your feet apart so that they are aligned with your shoulders.
- With palms up, raise both hands gradually, taking about 8 seconds to reach chest height.

- Begin to exhale.
- Turning the palms of your hands down, unlock the knees and let your hands fall gradually for about 8 seconds until they are naturally at your sides.
- The entire body should relax and become slightly lower in position as the hands drop.
- This body stature should be maintained throughout the practice of Tai Chi.
- The duration of inhalation and exhalation is determined by the depth of breath and the speed of movement; i.e., the slower the movement, the deeper the breath.
- You should practice combining movement and breath until it feels comfortable for you.
- Begin by inhaling for 4 seconds and exhaling for 4 seconds.
- You may then increase the duration of breathing by doubling or even tripling the amount of seconds, as

you decrease the speed of your movement.
- Deep breathing is good for overall health, but it should feel comfortable.
- Do not hold your breath.
- With the palms of your hands down and the fingers bent, try to align the two middle fingers on an imaginary line, parallel to and slightly above your waist.
- The hands should not be touching the body.
- Drop the wrist. Bend the knees slightly.
- The body weight should be evenly distributed on both feet.

2. STARTING TAI CHI

- Begin to inhale.
- Shift your weight to the left foot. Bring your right hand down, turning it so that the palm faces up. At the same time, bring the left hand up, palm facing down, as if you were holding a large ball in front of your body with two hands. Your head should be facing your left wrist. The left elbow should be dropped, wrists relaxed, the right arm bent. Do not bring the right elbow too close to the body. The left foot holds almost full weight of body. It is yang. The right foot holds almost no weight. It is yin. But, the right foot still fully touches the ground to retain balance.

- Begin to exhale.
- Reverse the rotation of both hands, as if you were rotating a large ball. The head should be facing the right wrist.
- Gradually shift your weight from the left foot to the right foot, alternating yin and yang, as the right foot becomes yang, and the left foot becomes yin.

- Shift your weight to the right foot, while gradually turning the shoulders to the right and raising the right arm up.
- The palm of right hand is facing down.
- At the same time, the palm of lower left hand is facing up.
- Do not bring the left elbow too close to the body.
- Again, you appear to be holding a large ball, head facing your right wrist.
- Full body weight is on the right foot, with the left foot touching the ground for balance.
- The right elbow is dropped, the right wrist is relaxed, and the left arm is bent in a smooth arc.

3. CATCH BIRD'S TAIL

- In this posture, there are four sub movements:

A. WARD OFF

- Begin to inhale.
- Keep your weight on the right foot, with almost no weight on the left foot.
- Turn your left foot slightly, clockwise, to be ready for the next move.

- Gradually shift your weight to left foot, while turning your shoulders and aligning the spine to face forward, and while rotating the left forearm counter-clockwise until the left hand is above the chest.
- At the same time, rotate your right forearm clockwise, lowering the right hand.
- The left elbow is dropped, left wrist is relaxed and hands open naturally.
- All moves described are done simultaneously

- With weight on left foot, move right foot to the side of left foot, touching the ground with the right foot's toes.
- Again, both hands appear to be holding an imaginary ball, with the left hand up, and the right hand down.
- The left elbow is dropped.
- Do not bring the right elbow too close to body.
- The head should be erect and facing forward.

- Begin to exhale.
- With the right foot, take one step to the right and slightly back, so that if an imaginary line were drawn from the heel of the right foot, the distance between the line and the left heel would be equal to the width of a fist.

- Gradually shift your weight to the right foot while simultaneously turning the shoulders to the front, raising the right forearm with your right palm facing the chest and lowering the left hand with your left palm facing down.
- The spine acts as an axle, with the shoulders turning around the spine, arms following shoulders, and hands following arms.
- Do not push out with the right arm, raise the right hand up, or drop the left hand down separately.
- All moves coordinate with the spine, and the spine must coordinate with the shift of weight.

- With the bulk of weight on right foot, turn your head and body slightly to the right.
- Holding the right forearm in front of the chest, drop the right elbow.
- Bend your left arm and press down with the left hand. Do not bring the left elbow too close to body.
- Keep your head erect, facing right.
- Do not stick out the chest or buttocks, and keep both feet firmly on the ground, as you look at a far away distant horizon.

B. PULL BACK

- Begin to inhale.
- While shifting your weight to the front (right) foot, the back (left) foot remains on ground to help balance body.
- Gradually lower left hand.
- Maintain head position.

- Imagining you are holding another's arm, rotate both forearms counter-clockwise, raising the right hand to above chest height, palm facing down, and the left hand to under chest height, palm open and upward.
- Maintain weight on the front foot with the back foot fully touching ground.
- Relax your shoulders.
- Drop elbows.
- Hold trunk of body erect.
- Maintain head position.
- Do not lean forward.
- Do not stick the buttocks out.

- Gradually shift your weight to the back foot, turning the shoulders to the left, as if you were pulling another person to the left side of your body, while trying to keep your hips facing front.
- The head faces down.
- The arms and hands move with shoulders, and the shoulders move with the shift of weight.
- Do not forcefully pull with the hands.
- Do not bring the right elbow too close to body.

C. SQUEEZE

- Begin to inhale.
- Raise right forearm rotating clockwise with the right palm facing your chest and rotate the left palm around the left wrist clockwise simultaneously to touch the end of your right forearm close to your right hand with the end of your left palm close to the left wrist.
- The head is turned toward the left, facing your hands.
- Keep the trunk of the body erect.
- Do not raise the shoulders.
- Maintain stable body height.

- Begin to exhale.
- Keep turning your shoulders to the left, trying to keep the hips facing front.
- Slightly press the end of right forearm close to the right hand with the end of the left palm close to the left wrist.

- Gradually shift your weight to the front foot, turning shoulders back to the right.
- Following shoulders, the right forearm enhanced with the left arm turns to the front as if to squeeze another person away.
- With this motion, you use the power of the rotating body, instead of hands.
- The head should be erect, facing right, the direction pointed to by right foot.

D. DOUBLE PUSH

- Begin to inhale.
- With your weight on the front foot, the left foot touching the ground for balance, turn the palms of both hands outward.
- Maintain head position.
- Do not lean forward.

- Keep your weight on the front foot and your back foot touching the ground.
- Maintain head position.

- Gradually shift your weight to the back foot while lowering both hands to the sides of your hips with your palms pressing down and then rotating the palms facing each other.
- With the shift of weight, the body carries arms and hands backward.
- The head faces forward.

- Keeping all your weight on the back (left) foot, raise both hands, palms facing up, as if you were holding something.
- Relax the elbows.
- Keep the trunk of your body straight.
- The head faces forward.
- Do not stick the buttocks out.
- Maintain stable body height.

Try to bring both elbows as close together as possible without touching (right view).

While bringing the elbows as close as possible, separate hands as far as possible, rotating the palms around the wrists, the right palm counter-clockwise, the left palm clockwise (right view).

- Begin to exhale.
- Gradually shift your body weight forward, rotating the hands so that the palms face upward.

- While continuing keeping to rotate hands, try to align middle fingers horizontally while dropping elbows.
- Maintain head position.
- Move the body forward.
- The body brings hands forward.
- Do not push with the force of the hands.

With head erect and in same position, put most of weight on your front foot (right foot) with the back foot touching the ground.

4. SINGLE WHIP

Begin to inhale.

- With no weight on the left foot, rotate left foot counter-clockwise to be comfortable for the next move.
- Turn shoulders to the left.

- Shift your weight to the left foot, rotating the right forearm clockwise and lower the right hand to hip height.
- Drop the left elbow down, rotating the left forearm and left palm clockwise, the right palm outward.
- Do not bring the tip of left middle finger higher than eyebrows.

- Turn shoulders to the left, bringing the arms and hands to left.
- Following the shoulders, drop the left elbow with the left palm at neck height rotating clockwise and move the right hand to the left side rotating the right forearm clockwise.
- Remember, hands follow arms, arms follow shoulders, shoulders rotate around the spine, with the spine acting as axle.
- The head is erect, facing left.
- With no weight on the right foot, rotate your right foot counter-clockwise to be comfortable.

- Begin to exhale.
- Gradually shift weight to your right foot, turning shoulders facing front, raising the right hand rotating the right forearm clockwise and lowering the left hand rotating the left forearm counter-clockwise.
- The head is erect, facing the right hand.

While shifting weight to your right foot, turn the shoulders to the right, rotating the right forearm clockwise and the left forearm counter-clockwise.

- With your weight fully on the right foot, turn your shoulders to the right, while trying to keep hips facing forward, twisting the spine.
- Maintain head position.
- The left arm follows the shoulders, left hand raised, rotating the left forearm counter-clockwise.
- Simultaneously, raise your right hand above the chest rotating the right forearm clockwise, palm upward.
- Move the left foot closer to the right foot for balance.

- Begin to inhale.
- Grasp imaginary the hand of another imaginary person with your right hand.
- Raise the right hand, flexing the wrist backward.
- Open and fully extend fingers on the right hand.
- Then close the fingers, rotating the right hand around the right wrist clockwise.

SINGLE WHIP

- Close your right palm, dropping the right elbow slightly and allow movement in the joint bones.
- Point to your right wrist with the left fingers.
- Your head faces the right hand.

- With your head facing your right hand, grasp imaginary the hand of another imaginary person, pointing to the right wrist with your left hand fingers, drop both elbows, keeping the trunk of the body straight.
- Weight remains fully on the right foot.
- Point to the ground with your left foot.

- Begin to exhale.
- Turn shoulders to face left.
- The head faces the left hand.
- The weight remains fully on the right foot.
- Move your left foot one step to the left and slightly back, toes pointing to the left, so that if an imaginary line were drawn from the heel of the left foot, the distance between the line and the right heel would be equal to the width of a fist.

- Gradually shift your weight to the left foot, turning your shoulders to the left, the direction pointed out by the toes of your left foot.
- The left arm extends outward, with the left palm rotating counter-clockwise.
- The right hand maintains a grasping position.

- With most of your weight on the left foot, drop your elbows, keeping the palm of left your hand in a vertical position, facing front.
- The left hand fingers are relaxed.
- Keep grasping with the right hand.
- Weight shift, the turning of shoulders, the expansion of the left arm, and the rotation of palm movements must be coordinated.
- The palm of the left hand is extended from turning shoulders and rotating the left forearm and palm, but not pushing. It is the power of the rotating body that removes the other person, not the force from the left hand.
- Maintain an erect head position facing the left hand.

5. TAKING HANDS ATTACK

- Begin to inhale.
- Maintain an erect head position facing the left hand.
- With weight fully on your left foot, release the right foot.

- Rotate your right foot clockwise to be ready for the next move.
- Turn your shoulders back to face forward, lowering the right and left hands.

- Shift your weight to the right foot, turning your shoulders to the right, lowering the right and left hands.
- With no weight on left foot, rotate left foot clockwise to be ready for the next move.

With most of your weight on the right foot, raise the left hand.

- Begin to exhale.
- The head remains erect, facing right.
- With your weight fully on the right foot, move the left foot closer to the right foot.

Shift your weight to left foot, turning your head and shoulders to the front, raising the left forearm, and lowering the right arm.

With your weight fully on the left foot, raise the right hand up under the left arm.

- Begin to inhale.
- Shift your weight to the right foot, rotating the right lower arm to bring the right hand up.
- Lower the left hand.

With your weight on the right foot, lower the left hand, and slowly turn your right hand clockwise.

- With your weight fully on the right foot, point to the ground with your left foot to support balance.
- Turn the shoulders to the left, pulling your arms out and back.
- Head faces left.

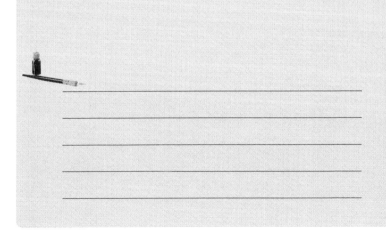

- Continue turning the shoulders to the left and looking back, as if you were backing up a car.
- Raise the left hand and lower the right hand, rotating the left arm counter-clockwise and dropping the left elbow.
- Maintain head position.

- Begin to exhale.
- Drop your left elbow, turn your shoulders to right, rotate the right forearm counter-clockwise.

- Keep turning your shoulders until you face forward. Bring the left arm forward.
- Maintain your weight on the right foot and keep the height of the body stable, avoiding any up and down movement.

- With weight on your right foot, and shoulders facing forward, the left foot supports body balance.
- Following the shoulders, move your left hand to the front, palm facing forward.

6. WHITE CRANE SPREADS WINGS

- Begin to inhale.
- With your weight on the right foot, turn the shoulders and head slightly to the right.
- Rotate your right forearm counter-clockwise to the chest, palm down.
- Try to keep your hips facing forward as you twist the spine, allowing each segment of the spine to move.

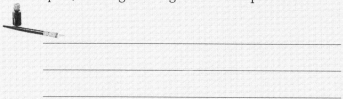

- With your weight on the right foot, return the head and shoulders to the front, rotating the right forearm and hand with palm up, clockwise to lower the hand to the side by your right hip.
- At the same time, rotate the left forearm clockwise to the chest, hand palm down.
- The head is facing forward and eyes are looking at the left wrist.

- Shift your weight to the left foot and turn your body slightly to the left.
- With the right hand by right hip and left hand in front of chest, turn right foot slightly counter-clockwise.

- Shift your weight to the right foot, turning the head and body to the left, with your right palm up and your left palm down, like holding an imaginary ball in front of body.
- The left foot points to the ground for balance.
- Maintain stable body height and look at the horizon.

- Keeping your weight on the right foot, the left toes pointing to ground, turn the shoulders to the right. Raise the right hand up to shoulder height, palm inward, rotating the right forearm clockwise.
- At the same time, lower the left hand, palm down, rotating the left forearm clockwise.
- The head faces the right hand.
- Do not raise the right hand too high.
- The right fingers should never be higher than the eyebrows.
- Maintain a stable body height.

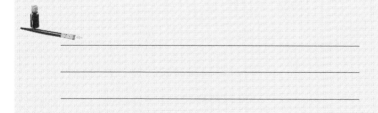

- Begin to exhale.
- With your weight on the right foot, turn your head and shoulders to the left, lowering the left hand, palm down, to your left hip.

- With your weight on the right foot, turn your head and shoulders to the left with right hand at neck height. The left hand is at your left hip, pressing down slightly, but not too close to the body.
- Left toes point to the ground to maintain body balance.
- The head is erect and facing forward.
- With eyes looking at the horizon, relax the chest and tuck in the buttocks.

7. RIGHT PUSH AND BRUSH KNEE

- Begin to inhale.
- With the knees slightly bent, your weight on the right foot, turn your shoulders to the left while rotating your right hand, palm inward, counter-clockwise toward the face.
- At the same time, rotate the left hand, palm outward, down to the left hip.
- Begin turning the head to left.

- Keeping your weight on your right foot, continue to turn your shoulders to the left, looking to the left, but keeping the hips facing forward, twisting the spine.

- With your weight on your right foot and the left toes pointing to the ground for balance, drop the right elbow and look at the tip of your right middle finger of the right hand.
- Turn the palm of the left hand to face inward.
- Maintain a stable body height (back view).

- With your weight on your right foot, shoulders facing forward, lower the right arm until the right hand reaches waist height and raise the left arm until your left hand reaches shoulder height.
- Eyes look at the middle finger of your left hand (back view).

- With your weight on the right foot, turn your shoulders to the right, and face right.
- Following your shoulders, right forearm and hand, rotate counter-clockwise until your right hand, palm inward, reaches neck height.
- The left forearm rotates to point to the right elbow with the left hand fingers.
- Eyes look at the middle finger of the right hand.

- Begin to exhale.
- With your weight on the right foot, move your left foot to the left and slightly back, so that if an imaginary line were drawn from the heel of the your left foot, the distance between the line and the right heel would be equal to the width of a fist.
- Start turning the shoulders to face forward with your right forearm and hand rotating counter-clockwise.
- At the same time, the left forearm and hand rotate clockwise until the left hand, palm facing downward, reaches waist height.

- Gradually shift your weight to the front (left) foot while continuing to turn the shoulders to face forward.
- Looking forward, rotate the right forearm counter-clockwise to locate the right hand, with the palm facing downward, at chest height.
- Rotate the left forearm clockwise to move the left hand, palm down, to the side of the left hip over the left knee, like attempting to brush away another, i.e. kicking foot.
- All movements should be in coordination with the spine, which acts as an axle.

- Continue shifting your weight to the front foot, rotating your right forearm and hand, palm outward, counter-clockwise until the right hand reaches waist height and then moves up to chest height, palm facing forward and the right elbow dropped.
- The left palm presses down slightly.
- Do not push the right hand too far.
- The pushing is powered by moving body weight instead of the force of the right hand.
- Eyes look at the horizon.
- The trunk of the body is held erect.
- The head position is maintained.
- Do not lean forward.
- Tuck in the buttocks.

8. PLAYING GUITAR

- Begin to inhale.
- With your weight on the front (left) foot, move back (right) foot forward slightly, to be ready for the next movements.
- Relax the wrists with your right hand, palm open, at chest height and left hand, palm inward, facing the side of your left hip.
- Eyes look to the horizon.

- Gradually shift your weight to the back (left) foot, lowering the right forearm to chest height with the palm of the right hand down and at the same time raising the left hand to waist height.
- Eyes look to the horizon.

- Keeping your weight on the right foot with the toes of your left foot left toes pointing to the ground for balance, drop the right elbow and raise the right hand to shoulder height, palm down relaxed and open.
- At the same time, raise your left hand to chest height, palm open and facing inward.
- Eyes look at left thumb.

- Begin to exhale.
- With your weight on the right foot, the left heel touches the ground to maintain balance.
- Begin dropping both wrists down and turning the palms up.
- Eyes look at left hand index finger.

PLAYING GUITAR

- With your weight on the right foot, your left heel points to the ground to maintain balance.
- Both wrists are dropped, with the palms of your hands open, turning up, naturally, at chest height.
- The palm of the left hand is in front of the palm of the right hand.
- Drop your elbows.
- Eyes look at left hand middle finger.
- Do not hold the right elbow too close to the body.

9. RIGHT PUSH AND BRUSH KNEE

- Begin to inhale.
- Keep your weight on the right foot, with the left heel pointing to the ground for balance.
- Raise both hands, palms up and open, to your face.
- Look at the the middle finger of the left hand.

- With your weight on the right foot, move the left foot to close to your right foot.
- Turn your shoulders to the right, look to the right, and lower your right forearm and hand to the side of your right hip.
- Raise the left forearm and hand to your chest.

- With your weight on the right foot, look to the right.
- Bend your right arm, raising the right forearm and hand, palm up and open, to full extension, so that the palm of the right hand faces your neck.
- At the same time, rotate the left forearm clockwise and point to the right elbow with the left hand fingers.

- Begin to exhale.
- With your weight on the right foot, move your left foot one step forward and slightly to the left, so that if an imaginary line were drawn from the heel of the left foot, the distance between the line and the right heel would be equal to the width of a fist.
- The heel of the left foot touches the ground for balance. Eyes look at the right hand.
- Rotate the right forearm and hand clockwise around the elbow, which is dropped and fixed at your side by your ribs.
- Lower the left forearm until the left hand reaches waist height.

RIGHT PUSH AND BRUSH KNEE

- Gradually shift your weight to the front (left) foot, with eyes looking at the horizon.
- Return the shoulders to face forward.
- Following the shoulders, lower the right forearm and hand, palm down, to waist height and then raise up to chest height.
- At the same time, lower the left forearm and hand, palm down, until the hand reaches the hip and then sweep your hand over the left knee, like brushing away another, i.e. kicking foot.

- With your weight on the front (left) foot, gradually turn your shoulders to face forward, extending the right arm and hand with palm open and facing forward naturally.
- Movement of the right hand forward is powered by the body, rather than by the force from the right hand.
- Move the left hand over the left knee, palm open and facing down.
- The left hand presses down slightly and pauses by left hip.

10. LEFT PUSH AND BRUSH KNEE

- Begin to inhale.
- Shift your weight to the front (left) foot.
- With no weight on the right foot, move the right foot forward and rotate it slightly, counter-clockwise, in order to be ready for the next movement.
- Look forward and relax both wrists.

- Shift your weight to the back (right) foot.
- Move the left foot close behind the right foot.
- Turn shoulders to the left, trying to keep your hips forward to twist the spine.
- Following the shoulders, the right forearm rotates counter-clockwise with the right elbow dropped, and the left forearm rotates clockwise to point to the right elbow with the left fingers.

- Shift your weight to the left foot and continue to turn the shoulders to the left, eyes looking to left.
- Following the shoulders, the left forearm rotates counter-clockwise, the left elbow dropped, with the left hand reaching the height of your shoulders.
- At the same time, the right forearm pivots at the elbow counter-clockwise, to point to the left elbow with the right hand fingers.

- Keeping your weight on the left foot, look at your left hand's fingers.
- Turn the palm of the eft hand inward; relax the right wrist (back view).

- Begin to exhale.
- With the weight on your left foot, move your right foot to the right and slightly back, so that if an imaginary line were drawn from the heel of the right foot, the distance between the line and the left heel would be equal to the width of a fist (back view)

- Gradually shift your weight to the front (right) foot, turning your shoulders to face forward.
- Extend the left arm rotating clockwise until the left hand reaches chest height.
- At the same time, lower the right forearm rotating counter-clockwise until the right hand is over the right knee, to the right side of your right hip, as if brushing away another,, i.e. kicking foot (back view).

- Continue shifting your weight to the front (right) foot and gradually turn your shoulders to face forward.
- Rotate your left forearm until the left hand reaches shoulder height with the palm of the hand facing forward, as if to push another person away.
- The push is propelled by the body movement, rather than by the force from the hand.

11. RIGHT PUSH AND BRUSH KNEE

- Begin to inhale.
- With your weight on your front (right) foot, move the left foot forward slightly, turning it slightly clockwise, to be ready for the next movement.
- Start turning your shoulders to the left, rotating the left forearm counter-clockwise to open the hand, palm up, and relax wrist.

- With your weight fully on left foot, move the right foot backwards, close to the left foot, while facing forward.
- Meanwhile, keep turning your shoulders to the right, raising the left forearm, dropping the left elbow and bringing the left hand, palm up and open, toward the face.
- At the same time, raise your right forearm rotating counter-clockwise with the right palm of the hand facing upward.

- Shift your full weight to the right foot, with the toes of the left foot pointing to the ground for balance.
- Turn your shoulders to the right.
- Following the shoulders, the right forearm rotates counter-clockwise and raises the right hand, palm open and facing inward, to neck height.
- The left forearm rotates clockwise and fingers of the left hand point to the right elbow.
- The head should be erect and facing the right hand.

- Begin to exhale.
- With your weight on your right foot, move the left foot one step to the left and slightly back, so that if an imaginary line were drawn from the heel of the left foot, the distance between the line and the right heel would be equal to the width of a fist.
- The head faces left, with eyes looking at the right hand. Rotate the left forearm and hand, palm down, clockwise and lower the left hand to waist height.
- Rotate right forearm and hand, palm open, counter-clockwise, right elbow dropped (back view).

- Gradually shift your weight to the front (right) foot, returning shoulders to the left, rotating the right forearm and hand, palm open and down, counter-clockwise until the right hand reaches chest height.
- At the same time, move left hand over the left knee to the side by your left hip, like brushing away another's kicking foot.

- With most of the weight on front (left) foot, and shoulders moving to face forward, eyes look at the horizon.
- Following the shoulders, lower the right forearm and hand, palm open and down, to waist height and then raise up to chest height.
- Finally, the right elbow drops, the forearm extends, the wrist flexes and the palm of the right hand faces forward, as if to push another person away.
- The power of body movement pushes the right hand forward, instead of the force from the right hand, itself. The left hand moves close to the left hip and presses down slightly.
- Hold the trunk of body erect.
- Do not lean forward.
- Relax the chest and tuck in the buttocks.

12. PLAYING GUITAR

- Begin to inhale.
- Shift your full weight to the front (left) foot, moving the back (right) foot forward slightly, to be ready for the next movement.
- Relax the wrists.
- Eyes look at the horizon.

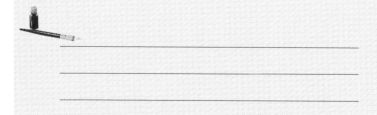

- Shift your weight to the back foot (right foot), drop the right elbow to lower the right forearm to just under your chest.
- With the right wrist relaxed, rotate the left forearm counter-clockwise to bring the left hand to the front gradually.
- Eyes look at the horizon.

Keep your weight on right foot, raise the right wrist to shoulder height and the left wrist to chest height.

- Keep your weight on the right foot with the left heel touching the ground for balance.
- Relax the wrists.
- Eyes look at the left hand thumb.

- Begin to exhale.
- With your weight on your right foot, the left heel touches the ground to maintain balance.
- Drop both wrists.
- Both hands are facing each other.
- Both palms are naturally open and facing each other.
- The left hand is in front of the right hand.
- Eyes look at the left middle finger.
- Do not let the right elbow be too close to the body.

13. SIDE PUNCH AND STRAIGHT PUNCH

- Begin to inhale.
- With your weight on the right foot, move the left foot close to the right foot, turning the left foot slightly, counter-clockwise.
- Relax the wrists.
- Head faces forward with eyes looking at the horizon.

- Shift your weight to the left foot, turning your shoulders to the left.
- Following your shoulders, the left forearm rotates clockwise until the left hand, with palm facing down, reaches chest height.
- At the same time, the right forearm extends and rotates counter-clockwise to waist height as the palm of your right hand forms a loose fist with a hole made by the fingers and thumb.
- Eyes look at left fingers.

- With your weight on the left foot, the right toes point to the ground for balance.
- Turn your shoulders to the left, with eyes looking at the left hand fingers.

- With your weight on the left foot, raise the left wrist to the left side of your chest and rotate the right forearm and hand counter-clockwise, moving the right fist under the left wrist.
- Eyes look at the left wrist.
- Do not let the right elbow be too close to the body (back view).

- Begin to exhale.
- With the right foot, take one step to the right and slightly back, so that if an imaginary line were drawn from the heel of the right foot, the distance between the line and the left heel would be equal to the width of a fist.
- Start to rotate the right forearm and fist clockwise (back view).

- Gradually shift your weight to the right foot, returning the shoulders to face forward.
- Rotate the right forearm and fist clockwise, extending the right arm.
- Rotate the left forearm and hand clockwise and point to the right elbow with the left fingers.
- The spine acts as an axle, with shoulders turning around the spine, arms following shoulders, and hands following arms (back view).

SIDE PUNCH AND STRAIGHT PUNCH

- Shift your full weight to the front (right) foot.
- The right forearm rotates clockwise, around the right elbow, with the right fist punching down.
- Keep your head erect, facing forward.
- Do not push out your chest or buttocks, and keep both feet firmly on the ground.

- Begin to inhale.
- Shift your weight to the back (left) foot, releasing the front right foot.
- Start turning the shoulders to the right, rotating the right forearm around the right elbow counter-clockwise until the right fist is in a vertical position.
- Eyes look at the horizon.

- Move the right foot back, close to the left foot, and turning it slightly clockwise.
- Shift your weight to the right foot, releasing the left foot, and turn your shoulders to the right, trying to keep the hips forward to twist the spine.
- Following your shoulders, the right arm moves to the right with the right forearm rotating counter-clockwise, the right fist becoming horizontal and close to chest.
- The left forearm and hand rotate clockwise.
- The head faces right.

- With your weight fully on the right foot, the left toes point to the ground for balance.
- Turn shoulders to the right, with eyes looking to right. Following your shoulders, the right arm extends and moves to the right, rotating the right fist counter-clockwise and horizontal.
- Extend and raise your left arm to above waist, rotating left hand counter-clockwise, palm facing outward.

- Begin to exhale.
- With your weight on the right foot, move the left foot one step to the left and slightly back, so that if an imaginary line were drawn from the heel of the left foot, the distance between the line and the right heel would be equal to the width of a fist.
- The head faces right.
- Rotate the right forearm and the fist counter-clockwise to extend to right side, and then rotate the right forearm and fist clockwise to return the fist to side of your waist with the fist horizontally upward.
- Raise the left forearm to chest height by rotating counter-clockwise leaving the palm of the left hand open and facing upward.

- Gradually shift the weight of your body to the front (left) foot, turning the shoulders to face forward, eyes looking at the horizon.
- Following the shoulders, extend the right arm, rotating the right forearm and the fist counter-clockwise.
- At the same time, the left forearm and hand rotate counter-clockwise until the hand, palm open and upward, reaches shoulder height.

- Keep shifting your weight until most weight is on your front (left) foot, while your eyes look at the horizon. Both feet touch the ground firmly.
- With weight shifting, rotate the right arm counter-clockwise and punch forward with your vertical right fist.
- The right fist is powered by the body movement of your spine, shoulders and arms, not by the force of the right hand.
- Keep the right elbow dropped, do not punch too far with the right fist.
- At the same time, the left hand rotates clockwise to move close to the right wrist, protecting the right hand.
- Hold the trunk of your body erect.
- Do not lean forward.
- Tuck in the buttocks.

14. CLOSING

- Begin to inhale.
- Shift your full weight to the front (left) foot, moving the back (right) foot forward slightly, with eyes looking at the horizon.
- Both hands at neck height open naturally.
- Drop the elbows.

- Shift your weight to the back (right) foot, keeping the head erect.
- Eyes look forward.
- Lower the hands, palms open and down, to waist height.

- Keeping your weight on the right foot, eyes look forward.
- With palms of the hands rotating upward to the face, gradually raise both hands to chest height.
- Try to bring both elbows as close together as possible and separate the hands as far as possible (left view).

- Begin to exhale.
- Move the left foot forward slightly.
- Gradually shift your weight forward, turning the right hand counter-clockwise and left hand clockwise, around the wrists.
- Try to drop the elbows (left view).

Keep shifting your weight, with eyes looking forward, turning the palms of the hands face down.

- Gradually keep shifting your weight to the front (left) foot, eyes looking forward.
- Turn hands so that the palms face forward.
- Try to align your two middle fingers on one imaginary line.

- With shifting of most of the weight to the front foot, the body brings palms of both hands forward.
- Do not push with the force of hands.
- Do not push too far.
- The palms of the hands open naturally.
- The head is erect, facing forward (left view).

15. CROSS HANDS

- Begin to inhale.
- Shift your full weight to the left foot, releasing the right foot, rotating it slightly around its heel, clockwise, turning your shoulders to the right.
- Following the shoulders, the body turns to the front, bringing the hands to the front with palms outward.

- With your weight fully on the right foot, turn the left foot around its heel clockwise, to have your body facing to front, and lower both hands to the sides of the hips.
- Do not push out the chest or buttocks, and keep both feet firmly on the ground, as eyes look at the horizon.

- Keep your weight evenly on both feet, raise both the hands up to chest height with the right wrist in front of the left wrist, and the palms of both hands open and facing inward, naturally.
- Eyes look at the horizon.

- Begin to exhale.
- With your weight evenly distributed on both feet, head erect, facing front, turn palms of both hands to face down, and lower both hands slowly to waist height.

- Lower both hands, with palms open naturally, to sides of hips.
- Eyes look at the horizon.

16. ENDING TAI CHI

- Breathe normally.
- Shift your weight to the right foot, releasing the left foot.

- With weight on the right foot, move the left foot close to the right foot.
- The body is erect, hands at your sides, in normal standing position.
- Tai Chi for Seniors exercise is now complete.

Made in the USA
San Bernardino, CA